W

OF
HIS WINGS
HELEN TEMPLE

Beacon Hill Press of Kansas City
Kansas City, Missouri

Copyright 2002
by Beacon Hill Press of Kansas City

ISBN 083-411-9587

Printed in the
United States of America

Cover Design: Paul Franitza

All Scripture quotations not otherwise designated are from the
King James Version.

Library of Congress Cataloging-in-Publication Data

Temple, Helen, 1914-
    Shadow of his wings / Helen Temple.
       p. cm.—(Helen Temple classics)
    ISBN 0-8341-1958-7 (pbk.)
      1. Christian converts—Biography. 2. Christian biography. I. Title.

  BV4930 .T46 2002
  248.2'46'0922—dc21
  [B]   2001043810

10   9   8   7   6   5   4   3   2   1

SHADOW
OF
HIS WINGS

CONTENTS

INTRODUCTION

THESE STORIES first written many years ago are presented to the readers as fresh and new as when they happened, with the prayerful hope that they may once again challenge us to "stake our lives" on the truth that God loves us and gave His life to redeem us from our sins. What else matters?

The story of Ahmed (not his real name), titled "The Search for Peace," originally ended with his conversion to Christ. To tell how he escaped those who sought his life would have, and still could, sign his death warrant. Therefore I have purposely imagined a reasonable but not factual means by which he could escape from the part of the world where he was known and where his life was at risk. I trust the readers will understand why in this case the truth is still too dangerous to print.

The story "Freedom!" is true and could be repeated many times as people have fled from an oppressive regime and in their flight have been met by Jesus, who gave them the true freedom they craved.

"Except a Corn of Wheat Fall" is a true story of a present-day miracle. It happened. And out of the tragedy that could not be explained in human terms, Koichi [Ko-EE-chee] saw precious young people redeemed and set free even in the hostile city of Taisha [Tah-EE-SHAH]—a stronghold of Satan.

Only eternity will reveal all the fruit that came from the precious "corn of wheat that fell" many years ago.

As we see the fruits of God's grace through the years, we are forcefully reminded that God indeed has a purpose in each of our lives that only eternity will reveal. He asks only that we believe when we cannot see—putting our faith totally, without any reservation, in Jesus Christ, the Son of God.

THE SEARCH
FOR PEACE

AHMED KAMAL [KAH-MAHL] MOVED IDLY
through the bazaar of the ancient Syrian city of Hama.
Being an officer in a large Mideastern army and a po-
litical figure of some importance in his country,
Ahmed was already familiar with many of the major
cities of the Middle East. His position in the government had taken him to most of them many times. To
while away his free hours on his journeys, he had tak-
en up the hobby of searching for unusual pieces of silver. Usually his free time was all too brief for the ex-
ploring he wanted to do. It was a pleasure for once to
have all the time he wanted.

As a loyal Muslim officer he had drawn a six-
month leave of absence to make his pilgrimage to
Mecca. This is the last of the five major achievements
required of all Muslims to assure them of paradise.

No duties demanded his time. He was traveling
with fellow officers and friends, all on the same mission and all with time to spend. They intended to

make the most of it, stopping in whatever places they fancied, staying as long as they found them interesting, and then moving on.

Sauntering through the Hama market, Ahmed glanced at the merchandise offered in the rows of narrow stalls, but he did not stop. His interest was in the silversmith's row, somewhere in the midst of the arguing, shouting shoppers that filled the streets.

Beyond the brass- and coppersmiths' booths Ahmed saw what he was searching for. At the very end of the row of metalworkers, he found a booth that showed promise. It had the unmistakable touch of the artist—an intricately designed, slender candlestick displayed by itself on a bit of black silk and a collection of three silver bowls arranged against a scarlet backdrop.

Ahmed stopped. *"Salaam alaikum* [Sah LAAHM Ah-LAH-eh-koom)," he said. "Peace be unto you."

"Wa alaikum es salaam," the shopkeeper answered, looking up from a slim silver case on which he was working. "And on you, peace."

Don't let me interrupt your work," Ahmed said. "I am only strolling through the bazaar."

The man nodded and went back to his work. Ahmed was surprised. Most men would have tried to sell him something. He stopped to watch the silversmith as he etched a finely traced design on the silver case.

"You do very beautiful work," he said impulsively, and immediately wished he hadn't. Now if he tried to buy the case, the man would undoubtedly double the price.

The silversmith looked up to acknowledge the compliment but said nothing.

"That's an interesting trinket you are working on," Ahmed said, hoping to sound less enthusiastic than he had at first. "What are you asking for it?" The silversmith looked straight at Ahmed. "This is a special order for an American gentleman," he said quietly. "It is not for sale."

Ahmed felt rebuked, for some reason, and walked away embarrassed and angry. The silversmith made no attempt to stop him. He went on working as though Ahmed had never been there.

Ahmed moved over to the next stall and examined some of the work there. The little silversmith took no notice of his going.

Slowly Ahmed moved back to the shop again. "Would you consider making a similar case for me," he asked. "I think something like this would be usable as a case for my cuff links and other small items when I travel."

"Can you work a design using my family insignia?" He removed a cuff link from his Western-style shirt. "This is the design, here on this link," he said, handing it to the silversmith. "I would like this to be the central part of the design."

The smith studied the design on the cuff link for several moments, then picked up a pencil and rapidly

sketched the crest, interwoven with a delicate design
of minute roses. He pushed it over to Ahmed.
"Something like this?" he asked.

Even in the rough sketch it was amazingly clear.

"That is excellent," Ahmed said, delighted.
"Ah—what do you ask for such an engraved case?"

The silversmith named a price so exactly right for
the value of the case that Ahmed was nonplussed.
The man was either a fool or disturbingly honest. But
since Ahmed had never known a shopkeeper to name
the price he wanted the first time, he decided the
man must be a fool.

"Too high!" he exclaimed, offering a ridiculously
low price instead.

The little silversmith looked at him steadily.
"You have already appraised my work with a knowledge above the average," he said quietly. "You knew
that my price was right. I knew that you knew. That
is why I did not try to bargain. The price I gave you
is what it is worth. If you wish me to make you a
case, I shall be glad to do so, but that will be the
price."

Again, Ahmed felt rebuked. But he knew that
the man was right. His recognition of Ahmed's
knowledge of values could be considered a compliment. He swallowed his pride and said, "I will take it
at your price. When can you have it finished?"

"I am not sure," the man replied. "It will take
me several days."

"Could you have it finished by Sunday?" Ahmed persisted. "We will stay here over our holy day, but on Saturday or Sunday at the latest, we should start on again. I am traveling with a party making a pilgrimage to Mecca," he added, with a trace of pride in his voice. "I must consider them too."

"I am not open on Sundays," the silversmith replied.

Ahmed recoiled. "An infidel!" he exclaimed hostilely.

"No, sir, a Christian," the man replied calmly.

Ahmed snorted, started to leave, then stopped. Infidel, Christian, Muslim—what difference did it make? He wanted the case. It was exactly what he needed, and the design was outstanding. He knew that he could never find another case that he would like as well.

"Monday, then?" he said. "Could you have it by Monday?"

"I will try," the silversmith replied. "Come by on Monday, and we will see."

Ahmed walked on through the bazaar. What was there about that silversmith that was so impressive? Ahmed shook his head, puzzled. In all his travels he had not met anyone who affected him as this man did.

The sun was sinking low in the western sky. Ahmed began to retrace his footsteps toward the inn. His companions would be waiting for him. When he entered the inn, the owner was bustling about, caring for his important guests. Servants were bringing the evening meal, placing bowls of steaming rice, roasted mutton, crisp cucumbers, and tomatoes on the table.

"You're late, my friend," his companions cried as he joined them. "Where have you been?"

"I know where he's been," a fellow officer said. "I've traveled with him before. He's been combing the bazaar, hunting for bargains. What did you find this time?"

Something made Ahmed want to keep silent about the little silversmith. "Nothing I would take with me," Ahmed answered. "I didn't have time to cover much of the market today."

"So we stay over another day!" one of the others said shortly. "What are the rest of us supposed to do? I've already seen all there is to see in the bazaar."

"Take a bus trip," another answered. "There are buses going to the historical ruins all day long. This place is famous for its ruins, you know."

With some dissatisfied grumbling the motley group of pilgrims eventually decided to stay on, tacitly acknowledging the leadership of the tall soldier who commanded their allegiance.

At the first sign of dawn the call of the muezzin [mew-EZ-zin, a Muslim leader who calls to prayer] from the top of the mosque brought Ahmed and his Muslim friends to their knees on their prayer rugs facing Mecca, the longed-for goal of their pilgrimage.

A handful of sweet, sun-ripened dates and two small whole wheat loaves with the strong black coffee of the Arab world was their breakfast.

Ahmed went again to the bazaar the next day. He fully intended to visit the other shops he had missed before, but he found himself threading his way through the crowds to the silversmith's shop, with an odd sense of anticipation.

"Peace be with you," Ahmed greeted the smith.

"And peace with you," the man answered.

The silversmith was working on the American's case.

He had an open book before him. Every once in a while he glanced at it, then appeared to be repeating some words softly under his breath.

Ahmed watched curiously. "What is it that you read as you work?" he asked, finally.

The smith smiled. "Oh, I'm not just reading," he said. "I am memorizing the words of Jesus from the Bible. This is a beautiful passage spoken by Jesus." He quoted: "Peace I leave with you, my peace I give unto you: not as the world giveth, give I unto you. Let not your heart be troubled, neither let it be afraid" (John 14:27).

"Why do you waste time learning the words of a minor figure like Jesus?" Ahmed asked. "Why don't you learn from the wisdom of the Koran—the words of our great prophet, Mohammed?"

"We believe that Jesus was the Son of God," the

shopkeeper said confidently. "There can be no greater words than His. He was crucified for our sins and was raised by God and is alive in heaven today. I have proved that this is true."

Ahmed was repelled by the sheer audacity of the man. "How can you believe such things to be true?" he demanded.

"Because the peace He promised He has given to me," the silversmith answered. "It's in my heart. It fills my life. I have known bad times, good times, times of sorrow, of bereavement, of sickness—but none of these has been able to disturb the peace that He gives."

Ahmed looked at the man, perplexed. Ordinarily, he would have cursed him and walked away. But what did one do in the face of such outrageous confidence? He had the uncanny feeling that if he had raised his arm to strike the man, it would have frozen in midair —or fallen to his side paralyzed. He turned away and lost himself in the crowd.

All through the day he thought about the silver-smith's words. He was angry with himself for being disturbed. Why should a simple workman trouble him so? What could he know about religion and truth? But what the man said about his peace was true. It was reflected on the man's face.

On Monday he went back to the shop to pick up his silver case. It was early. The shopkeeper was just opening up. No other customers were about. Ahmed could see the man's Bible lying open on the shelf.

"Peace be with you," Ahmed said, putting out his hand as he would to a friend.

"And peace with you," answered the silversmith. "Your case is finished," he said. He placed it on the counter in front of Ahmed.

It was beautiful. Every line, every leaf, every petal of the tiny roses was perfect. Every detail of the family insignia was reproduced exactly.

"Excellent!" he breathed. "The price?" Now was the time for the man to bargain if he wished to.

"The same as I told you before," the silversmith said quietly.

Ahmed paid him, and the man started to wrap the case.

"Wait!" Ahmed said. "I would like to look at some of your other pieces."

He looked at several of the items on display, only half seeing them. Then he leaned across the counter and said in a low, tense voice, "That Book!" He motioned to the Bible. "What makes you think it is true?"

"Because through it God speaks to my heart," the silversmith answered. "Why don't you read it for yourself and see?"

Ahmed looked quickly around. None of his friends were in sight. "I would like to," he said in a low voice. "Do you have another copy of this Book that I could borrow?"

At this the shopkeeper reached under the

counter and pulled out a small New Testament. "Here, take this," he said. "Read it, and you will know that what I say is true."

Ahmed slipped the Book into his inner pocket. "Keep my case here for another day or two, would you?" he asked. "I will come back to get it."

He walked away. Where could he go to read the Book? Not to the inn, that was sure. Not anywhere in the marketplace. The tourist bus—that would be the place! He hurried to the central hotel where the bus trips began and bought a ticket. Once at the ruins, he told the driver he would wait for a later bus and went in search of a secluded spot away from the usual tourist paths.

All that day Ahmed read from the little New Testament. The Holy Spirit spoke through His Living Word. As the time drew near for the last busload to return to the inn, Ahmed closed the Book. "This is Truth," he acknowledged. "But if I accept it, it will cost me everything I have, perhaps even my life." Slowly he made his way to the bus.

The next morning he went again to the silversmith's shop just as he was opening for business.

"Peace be with you," Ahmed said.

"And peace with you," the silversmith answered. He eyed Ahmed keenly.

"I have no peace," Ahmed said abruptly. "This Book you gave me bites like a serpent."

"Only if you reject it," the shopkeeper answered,

leaning over the counter. "Accept its truth, and it will make you free. Free from fear. Free from your hunger and longing for truth, for you will have found it. This is what you have been searching for, isn't it?"

"You don't realize what you are suggesting," Ahmed objected. "I am a high-ranking officer in my country's army. People look up to me. If I accept this Book as truth, I am doomed. My career is wrecked. They will follow me to the ends of the earth to kill me."

"Do you believe the words of the Book?" the silversmith asked.

"Yesterday as I read it—I did. Today—it is too much. I don't dare to believe it."

"If you believe the words of this Book, you already know that your soul is doomed for eternity if you don't accept it," the shopkeeper answered quietly.

"But the price!" Ahmed groaned. "The price of this belief. It is not humanly possible to pay it."

"Not alone. But with God it is possible," the silversmith answered. "Come inside my shop, and we will pray."

Quickly the shopkeeper replaced the shutters on the stall and closed it as though for the night. Inside, behind the boxes and piles of trade materials, the little Christian silversmith and the proud Muslim army officer knelt on the dusty floor to pray.

When they rose from their knees, the floor was wet with tears, but the peace on Ahmed's face was unmistakable. He shook hands with the silversmith.

"You may not see me again," he said. "But if you don't, you can know I will meet you in heaven. I shall tell my friends today that I am not going to Mecca and why. After that—," he shrugged his shoulders. "There are a thousand ways to get rid of an infidel. I know—I've used some of them."

The silversmith nodded. "I know that. But remember, 'Greater is he that is in you, than he that is in the world' [1 John 4:4]. You will never be alone."

He reached under the counter. "Your case," he said, handing it to Ahmed. Ahmed shook his head. "The insignia on that case will mark me for death," he said. "Will you keep it here for the present? If I succeed in getting safely away, I shall try to find someone to pick it up for me."

"God bless you and go with you," the silversmith said. "If I can help you, you know where to find me."

Back at the inn the others were just finishing breakfast. "Where have you been?" They demanded.

"Checking on an item I had seen earlier," Ahmed answered. "I didn't take it."

"Are you ready to leave now, Ahmed?" called one of the men. "We really should be getting on our way."

"You can start on anytime," Ahmed answered quietly. "I am not going any farther."

"You're not what?" His friends surrounded him in consternation. "What do you mean you're not going? What have you found in this place to change your mind?"

"It's a woman!" cried one. "I'm sure of it. That's what always makes fools of strong men."

Ahmed brushed their words aside. "No woman," he answered.

They stared at him as though he were out of his mind.

"I was going to Mecca seeking peace and assurance of heaven," he said. "But I have already found the peace of God, and His assurance of heaven. I don't need to go to Mecca."

He took the New Testament from his pocket. "Through the truth in this Book, I have believed in Jesus Christ as the Son of God, and He has given me peace."

"An infidel!" one cried, choking out the words. "Ahmed, you are insane."

"No, I am sane for the first time in my life."

"He's joking!" one of the officers laughed hollowly. "He wants to see what we will say. Get rid of that thing before someone believes you." He snatched at the Testament, but Ahmed held it away.

"I'm serious," Ahmed said, putting the Testament back in his pocket. "I am a believer in Christ. I am not going to Mecca."

They believed him then and cursed him with terrible oaths.

Friends pulled him aside. "You can't do this,

Ahmed," one of them said. "Think of your family. Your career. Even your life. You know what we do to infidels. You will never get out of this city alive. Tell the man you were joking. Come on with us to Mecca —and throw that cursed Book away."

Ahmed put his hand on his friend's shoulder. "I appreciate your desire to help me, friend," he said. "But I have thought this all through. I mean what I have said. This Book is Truth." He touched the pocket where he had placed the Testament. "I am not going to Mecca. I have already found the peace of God. It is greater than any human kind of peace could ever be."

His companions might have killed him where he stood, but the innkeeper, who had overheard the conversation, came running and pulled Ahmed away, pushing him into his own quarters.

"You'll have to leave at once," he said, hustling Ahmed through the rooms and out the small back door. "I don't know what you have done, but it will ruin my business if there is any violence in the inn." He thrust Ahmed into the alley and bolted the door after him.

Well, I'm still alive, Ahmed thought ruefully as he slipped from alley to alley until he was able to lose himself in the throngs of a crowded thoroughfare on the far side of the city. But this was not the end, he knew. His former friends would comb the city to find him. From this day on everywhere he went, someone would be looking for him, ready to earn merit with Allah by destroying an infidel.

Grateful that he was familiar with the city of Hama from previous visits, he made his way to a shabby inn whose owner was more interested in cash than credentials, and rented a small room. He settled in to wait until he was sure his friends had gone on to Mecca.

Only then did he cautiously make his way across the city to the silversmith's shop.

The smith greeted him warmly. "You are still alive!" he said. "God be praised! But we must get you away. Come to this address tonight. It is where Christians meet. He handed Ahmed a slip of paper and turned to greet other customers. When Ahmed arrived at the address that night, he realized that the Christians had been at work. They provided him with a worn traveler's burnoose (a hooded robe) and a cheap suitcase. "Don't be afraid to pull the hood forward to shadow your face. And shave your mustache," they said. The smith handed Ahmed a small silver pin shaped like a fish. "This will pass as a souvenir for a child," he said. "But will also identify you as a Christian if the need arises."

"You have probably been too busy to hear the news. Israel has just declared its independence as a nation. Everything is in chaos. This may be your salvation. The Arabs are fleeing from Israel. We've heard that many are going to Jordan, among them a group of Arab Christians. If we can smuggle you into the refugees fleeing to Jordan, go to Amman. Ask there for Christians. Join them, and watch for your chance to travel with any who may be going on to a safer part of the world. I don't know what kind of transportation you will find, but hopefully there will be something. Our prayers will be with you. He embraced Ahmed warmly and bid him farewell.

The chaos in the new nation of Israel was already being felt in Syria and other border states, as the refugees sought shelter. Not every nation welcomed them, and many were continuing their flight toward Jordan. Ahmed joined the groups, walking, catching transportation where he could find it. It took him days to make it across the Jordan border and on to the city of Amman. Christians were still scarce enough that their whereabouts were known, and Ahmed found the group he was seeking. He joined them, awaiting his chance to escape to Europe without drawing attention to himself.

It was many months later when a stranger came to the silversmith's shop in Hama.

"A friend of mine is leaving in a few weeks to go overseas," he said. "When he learned that I was coming to Hama, he asked if I would pick up a package he had left here with you."

He held out a silver pin shaped like a fish. "My friend said that this would let you know who he was."

The silversmith took the pin, turned it over, and

studied the tiny initials he had engraved there long ago.

He went to the back of the shop and took a package wrapped in brown cloth from a high shelf. "I took the liberty of making a few changes," the silver-smith said. "I think your friend will like them. It will make it more useful. Give this to your friend with my greetings, and may God grant him a safe journey."

Not until the traveler had delivered the package several weeks later did Ahmed realize what the changes were. The family insignia, which would have identified Ahmed anywhere, was now disguised. Additional engraving covered the original design with an ornate cross and a crown, displayed against the stylized rays of the sun, with a tiny dove flying aloft. It was impossible to discern the earlier pattern.

As Ahmed looked at the design that was now obviously Christian, he was amazed. "Beautiful!" he exclaimed. "I would not have believed it was possible!"

With a full heart he wrapped the case again in its brown cloth. *Thank God!* he thought gratefully. *Thank God for the little silversmith who introduced me to the Prince of Peace and started me on my journey to a life in His service.*

2

FREEDOM!

MRS. CHANG LOOKED OUT at the darkening sky. The clouds were a good omen. They would be needed tonight. She went to the heavy wooden chest and opened it. Her fingers caressed the bright lengths of silk cloth that she had bought for new quilt covers. *Who will get them now?* she wondered. She lingered over each one, then put it aside. At last she chose a scarlet and gold design and spread it on the floor. This one she would take. On it she laid two dresses and a change of underclothing.

She looked about her. What else could she take? What must she leave of these treasures of two generations and more? A tear trickled down her cheek, and she wiped it away. She went to the kitchen. The big, round cooking wok must stay. It couldn't possibly be carried in a bedroll. The wooden chopping board must be left also, and her charcoal brazier.

At last she chose her big chopping knife and two small rice bowls. These, with their chopsticks, would have to do. Wrapping the knife in paper, she placed the things in the center of the length of cloth on top of her clothing. She looked around the rooms once more, seeing each dear, familiar object with eyes that were looking on them for the last time. At the god shelf she stopped. Would she dare to take the images? No. If anyone came to the house, he or she would miss the gods immediately and would know that she and her husband had left for good. But how could she set out on such a perilous journey without the gods' protection?

At last she chose her favorite, an old image that had been hers for many years, and rearranged the others so that this one would not be missed. She rolled the little idol in a piece of cloth and added it to the other things. An extra pair of soft scuffs, a small bag of herbs, and one of tea completed her collection. She folded in the sides of the cloth and rolled the bundle neatly together. Then she replaced it in the chest.

Walking swiftly from window to window in their small house, she peered out into the street and then toward the houses that crowded in close beside theirs. No one seemed to be watching.

Mrs. Chang went back to the chest, removed a second piece of silk, and spread it on the floor. On it she quickly laid her husband's best padded *i shang* [EE-shahng, a robe worn by men], another one for summer, and his slippers. She looked with longing at the parchment and silk wall scroll that was his prized work in Chinese lettering, but she did not dare to take it down. It would be too obvious if it were missing. Much depended upon their being as far as possible on their way before it was discovered that they had gone.

She turned from the parchment and selected the soft camel hair brushes that were the tools for Mr. Chang's trade as a writer of fine Chinese script. She added a small sack of rice for the journey and folded in the edges of the cloth as before, rolling it into a neat bundle. This she also placed in the chest.

Preparations finished, she went to the kitchen and put on the rice and vegetables for her husband's supper.

When Mr. Chang came in from his work, he closed the door carefully and sat down by the table. Mrs. Chang lit the small oil lamp and brought him his supper.

To any passerby who might have been curious enough to look through the cracks in the loosely shuttered windows, it was a domestic scene no different from that in most of the houses on the narrow street. But in soft tones, not intended to reach beyond the walls of the room, Mr. and Mrs. Chang spoke to each other.

"Is it tonight?" Mrs. Chang asked.

"Tonight," Mr. Chang answered without looking at her. "Is everything ready?"

"I have packed what I could," she said, pouring him another cup of tea.

"What about the vegetables?"

"I hid them in baskets by the kitchen wall where no one can see."

"No one saw you get them?"

"No, I was weeding and covered them with weeds as I worked."

"Good. All must appear as though we are coming back soon. I left a fine piece of work unfinished at the shop and the brushes I was using as well. They know how I prize my brushes. No one would expect me to leave without those." He wiped his mouth and burped appreciatively for the good meal.

He picked up a book and began to read, as he usually did in the evening. But his mind took in nothing of what he saw on the pages. Over and over he traced in his mind the route of escape that he had been given. It could not be drawn on paper, lest it fall into the hands of the guards. It had to be memorized.

Now that the hour had come, he was tense and nervous. Everything was at stake in this venture. Leaving China, the land of his ancestors, meant that he could take nothing with him of all that he valued. It meant giving up his old work, his home, and most of his possessions.

Fortunately, he was not as wealthy as some who had left. He had nothing in the bank to leave behind as they did.

But there were great risks, even for him. Fleeing from China, without applying for permission to leave from the Communist officials, meant that if he were caught, he would be imprisoned and probably killed.

For a fleeting moment he was tempted to give

up the whole plan. It was not too late. Nothing was lost—yet.

But as he thought of the night classes in Communism, the "supervisors" who constantly inspected the shop where he worked, the increasing pressure to confess his shortcomings and betray a friend or associate as a traitor to the government, his heart recoiled. He could not stoop to that, but unless he did, he knew he must go—and now, while it was still possible. Already he was afraid he was under suspicion, because he had not "talked" to any of the authorities. Sooner or later he would be summoned to answer questions about his loyalty. Then it would be too late to flee. They must go now.

In the next room Mrs. Chang unfolded their quilts and spread them on the wooden bed.

Mr. Chang closed his book and blew out the lamp. They lay down, tense and silent, listening for any sound that might reveal that their plan had been discovered.

Gradually the street noises lessened. One by one the lights in other houses along the street flickered out. All was still except for the droning chirp of the crickets outside in the garden.

Mr. Chang sat up. "It is time!" he whispered.

Mrs. Chang rose and opened the chest. She took out the two bundles she had prepared earlier and rolled each one up in a sleeping quilt. She handed her husband a faded coolie outfit, and she herself put on the dingy blue trousers and short jacket of a hard-working countrywoman. They rubbed dirt from the garden on their bare feet to make them look as though they had walked a long way. Then Mrs. Chang put the blanket rolls across her shoulders, and her husband helped her tie them securely. From beneath the pile of weeds behind the kitchen wall he drew two shallow baskets filled with fresh Chinese cabbage, turnips, and melons and hung them on a carrying pole across his shoulders.

Pulling the door of the house softly shut behind them, Mr. Chang set out in the dense blackness of the moonless night. Mrs. Chang plodded six feet behind him, trying not to hurry. She must remember to look like a weary farm woman trudging behind her husband to the market.

Counting the streets silently to himself, Mr. Chang turned right, then left, and then left again, so many times that Mrs. Chang was completely lost.

It seemed to her that they had walked miles in the darkness. She longed to catch up with her husband and ask him how close they were to their rendezvous with the others, but she did not dare. Everyone knew that China had eyes in the night, everywhere, these days.

She trudged on, head down, plodding in earnest now, for her feet ached from the rough streets and the hours of walking.

The soft sound of waves lapping against the

shore reached her ears. They were near the riverfront. This was a danger point. Guards would be everywhere.

Other peddlers were on the streets now. Farmers were coming in from the country to sell vegetables and rice to the boats; coolies were coming with their wares. The Changs mingled with them but did not get close enough to be scrutinized. They moved through the first early arrivals and continued on, losing themselves in the darkness. Other boats were tying up along the riverbank, and more would be coming in with the dawn. It was natural for some of the coolies to go on down to the river to meet them.

When they had passed from the sight of the others, Mr. Chang hastened his steps until his wife had to trot to keep up with him.

The first faint signs of dawn began to show. In the dim light they saw the shape of a fishing boat drawn up to the shore. Men were working on their gear, loading it into the boat. Mr. Chang stopped. "We are here," he said in guarded tones.

The boatman motioned for them to get aboard. Mr. Chang hid his carrying pole and baskets under the bushes along the bank. Stumbling with weariness, he helped Mrs. Chang clamber over the side of the boat. They crept under the woven straw shelter in the center and huddled down as inconspicuously as possible.

The fishermen continued their preparations as though nothing out of the ordinary was happening.

At last all was stowed away to their liking. The men climbed aboard and pushed the boat away from the bank, poling until they reached deep water. There the boatman started his diesel motor and the heavy, seagoing fishing junk moved downriver, threading its way between the sampans and riverboats that were already beginning their day's activities.

Not daring to speak, the Changs sat in tense silence as the boat drifted almost within touching distance of the river traffic. The cloudy skies were in their favor, delaying the coming dawn those extra few precious moments that enabled the boat to reach the broad mouth of the river and start out into the open bay before it was fully light.

Once in the bay they breathed a little easier, though there was still much traffic in the harbor from outgoing fishing boats and the river travelers.

At last they left the harbor behind them and headed for the open sea. Other fishing boats fanned out, hailing each other as they passed, each one maneuvering to reach its favorite fishing spot before someone else.

The men on the Changs' boat went about their routine calmly, readying their lines and nets and preparing to cast them out when they reached the proper spot.

They moved out beyond most of the other fishing vessels, then cast out their lines, still within sight of the rest. Cutting the motor down to trolling speed, they moved back and forth in wide sweeps, each one taking them farther out.

An occasional reconnaissance plane patrolling overhead would not see anything unusual in this. Indeed, some distance away other boats were doing the same thing.

When the escape vessel was at the point where the boats usually turned back toward the harbor, the boatman switched his motor to high speed and turned the nose of the craft directly away from the mainland and toward the Ta Ch'en [Tah-CHEN] Islands. His men swiftly drew in their lines, and the powerful motor drove the boat ahead toward the distant islands and safety.

Guiding his craft with a practiced hand, the boatman glanced back over his shoulder toward the receding shores of China. His anxious eye took in the movement of boats on the water and scanned the sky for planes. Every moment they were undetected was a long step toward safety. The reconnaissance planes were up, flying their second patrol of the bay area. He watched as they flew their wide arc over the bay and back to shore. Safe for a moment! They had not been seen.

The boat labored steadily on, putting miles between them and China. The distant Ta Ch'ens were a faint streak on the horizon.

Again the reconnaissance planes appeared on patrol. As the boatman watched them, he saw one drop out of the flight pattern. Gradually it became larger.

It was moving their way. They were too far from the fishing grounds to fool anyone, but he decided to try. Switching the motor to trolling speed, he ordered the men to roll out the lines.

The plane came in low and made a pass over them as the fliers peered out the window. It circled around and came in again. The boatman looked up and waved. As he did, he caught sight of the machine guns. He shouted a warning, and the men dove for shelter. He snapped the motor into full speed and began a zigzag pattern. The plane swept over, machine guns blazing. Bullets spattered around them on the deck and in the water. It came once more, and the bullets whistled past on every side. Then the plane lifted in a long, lazy arc and went back to rejoin its companions.

The fishermen came out of hiding and checked the damage. Bullets had struck the wood frame of the boat in many places. Some had pierced the straw roof at a shallow angle, but miraculously, no bullets punctured the hull and no one was injured.

The boatman grimly held the boat at high throttle, watching over his shoulder for the possible return of the hunters. The fishermen rolled in the lines and took their places, looking for the island harbor on the distant shoreline ahead.

Late in the afternoon they reached the Ta Ch'ens. The boat slipped into the crowded harbor and tied up at the pier. Stiffly the Changs climbed out and made their way along the pier to the shore. Tears ran down Mrs. Chang's cheeks—tears of relief for the safe journey and tears of grief for the land and memories they had left behind them.

They found a cheap inn and engaged a room, while they tried to decide what to do next. Somehow they had to find a way to build a new life—here in the Ta Ch'ens or somewhere else.

The Changs had been on the island only a few days when they were awakened one morning by the droning sound of many planes. They sprang from bed and ran to the street. People were streaming from the buildings. Everyone looked toward the mainland. High in the early morning sky planes were coming, flying in formation. For a stunned, unbelieving moment the people were rooted to the spot. Then someone shouted, "Bombers! Run!" and the crowd scattered. The Changs followed them to the nearest bomb shelter. They were scarcely inside before the bombs began falling.

The planes passed over in waves, dropping their bombs and circling to come back low and strafe the area with machine guns. Then they wheeled away and returned to the mainland.

Slowly the people crept out of the shelters. They looked around them with surprise. Few of the buildings in the center of the town were damaged. But then they looked toward the harbor. The docks were in chaos. Boats listed at odd angles or settled leadenly in the water. Some had sunk completely. The larger vessels anchored out in deep water had taken the worst of the attack. Most were sunk or burning. Many of the people who had been on the boats were dead or injured. Few boats had been missed.

The owners of the few craft still afloat moved them away from the docks to whatever makeshift shelter they could find, camouflaging them with tarpaulins and tree branches. Others went to see what they could salvage.

Fear gripped the hearts of the Changs. If the Communist soldiers invaded the Ta Ch'ens, the Changs knew that they themselves and the other refugees would be the soldiers' first victims.

"We must leave here," Mr. Chang said. "We must get to Taiwan as soon as possible."

He haunted the shipping offices until he secured passage for himself and his wife on a small vessel that was returning to Taiwan.

They left at night, hoping to put as much distance as possible between them and the Ta Ch'ens before morning.

As the sky began to brighten in the east, the captain of the ship took refuge in the lee of a small, wooded island. He shut off his motor, and with poles the crew pushed the vessel under the branches of a tree that hung over the water. They knew the planes would be on the lookout for ships, and the pilots' eyes were keen.

They saw waves of planes come over for the daily bombing of the Ta Ch'ens. They saw them circle in widening arcs, scanning the sea below. Then they saw one plane swing away from the rest and head in their direction.

Everyone scrambled for shelter. The plane swooped low, following the shore of the wooded island where they were hidden. Twice it circled the small bit of land, before going on its way back to the mainland of China.

"We are safe," the captain said. "I don't think they will be back today, but we will wait until dusk to be sure."

As the sun sank below the horizon, the captain and his crew pushed the ship out from its shelter, started the diesel motor, and began their long trip to Taiwan and safety.

At first they skirted the scattered small islands, keeping them between them and the mainland.

When the last island was behind them, the captain opened the throttle as wide as he dared and headed into the open sea. From here on there would be no refuge until they reached the safety of Taiwan. By the time dawn brightened the eastern sky, they were near enough to Taiwan to hope for their protection if enemy planes came over.

The ship finally dropped anchor in the Taiwan harbor of Chi-lung, and the Changs stepped ashore. They had nothing with them but their bedrolls, but they were safe, and they were free. That was worth everything.

They found a temporary room, and in a short time Mr. Chang had secured a position as bookkeeper in a local high school.

Slowly and painfully they began to rebuild their shattered lives. A few friends, refugees like themselves; a new god to add to the only one they had dared to bring; the purchase of a book—little by little they added substance and meaning to the new life they had begun to live.

They had been in Taiwan for several years when a stranger who came to call one day interrupted the quiet ordinariness of their lives. He introduced himself as the pastor of the Church of the Nazarene. It was a strangely foreign name, and it did not attract Mrs. Chang. Taiwan had many people and places with strange-sounding names these days.

But the stranger was warm and friendly, and his sincerity was real. Over a cup of tea Mrs. Chang found herself asking questions about the church with the foreign-sounding name and liking the answers. When the pastor left that day, Mrs. Chang had the warm feeling that she had found a friend who cared.

She welcomed the pastor's visits, and as the weeks passed she found herself voicing her anxious fears concerning her husband's activities that took him away evenings—for gambling or worse.

The church people became her friends, and

eventually Mrs. Chang accepted their invitation to worship with them. Little by little their warm Christian love drew her in until one day she reached out and accepted Christ's love for herself.

She was happier than she had ever been before in her life. But there remained one point of sadness, which even her newfound faith could not assuage. They had had no children. When they were fleeing from the mainland, it had been a blessing not to have small children to care for; but now, in this free land, Mrs. Chang longed again to have a child. If she could not bear one of her own, then she wished she could find one that someone else did not want.

Providentially, shortly after her conversion, someone told Mrs. Chang of a poor fisherman and his wife who were looking for someone to take their year-old baby daughter. They had a large family and felt they could not rear this last one.

The Changs quickly made contact with them. One glimpse of the tiny, doll-like little girl and their hearts were captured. They arranged to adopt the child. They named her "Summer's Breath," and indeed she was sweet and refreshing to both of them.

Mr. Chang cautiously accepted the Christian way of life soon after the little girl came to live in their home. At first he did well, bringing little Summer's Breath to church and teaching her to pray as soon as she could lisp a few words. But faith was difficult for this practical-minded businessman to grasp. He often found himself fretting over their financial problems. Hearing him, little Summer's Breath would ask in surprise, "Aren't you going to ask God what to do? He knows."

Summer's Breath was an amazing little girl. Before she was old enough to go to kindergarten, she was singing the hymns of the church from memory. She gave her heart to Christ while she was a very small child, and her faith in God seemed limitless.

There were times when the Changs were a little hesitant to speak of their Christian faith to their Buddhist friends, but it was not so with Summer's Breath. Everyone in the city knew that she was a Christian. She talked about Jesus as one would talk about a dear friend.

But while his daughter was letting the beauty of God shine through her life, Mr. Chang was becoming less and less active in the Christian way. Business pressures gradually pulled him away. He began to smoke and to seek entertainment in places that he knew did not please God.

When Summer's Breath was 11 years old, she became ill. At first her mother thought it was a common childhood ailment. She treated her with the usual home remedies they had used all their lives. But Summer's Breath did not get any better.

After many months they took her to a doctor. He diagnosed her illness as a skin disease. When she did not respond to his treatment, they took her to other doctors. But she became steadily worse. Finally she was unable to eat at all.

Doctors gave her blood transfusions, medicines, and nourishing food. The missionary anointed her with oil and prayed for her to be healed if it was God's will.

At last the doctors told Mr. and Mrs. Chang that there was no hope for Summer's Breath's recovery.

The grief-stricken parents stayed by their daughter's bed. Mrs. Chang committed her little girl to God's care, her aching heart trusting Him to do what was best. Heavyhearted, Mr. Chang longed for the faith in God that his wife and daughter had.

One day as her parents watched beside her, Summer's Breath opened her eyes and said, "I am going to be with Jesus soon. I'll be waiting for you." She looked at her father. "Papa, what about you?"

"I'm not ready," he said weeping. "I know I've displeased God."

Bowing beside his little daughter's bed, Mr. Chang confessed his failure and asked God for forgiveness. With tear-filled eyes he promised little Summer's Breath that he would live for God so that one day they could all be together again.

Summer's Breath died a few days later. A simple stone cross was placed above her grave, proclaiming to all who passed by that a sweet little girl was now in heaven with her Savior. And the Changs are faithfully telling their friends that one day they, too, will be

joining their little girl in heaven, never to be separated again.

3

Except a Corn of Wheat Fall

I SHALL NEVER FORGET the day God called me to preach the gospel in the city of Taisha.

Taisha, Japan, is the headquarters of Shintoism. Its name means "big shrine," and it is named for the great Shinto shrine, which was built there about two thousand years ago.

Shinto worshipers believe that 80 million gods meet in Taisha for their general assembly each year during the month of November. There is a big hotel where the gods are supposed to stay.

No one can go outside his or her home nor open a door or window on the first day of November, because that is the day the gods come and anyone who sees them will be blinded.

The hostility of the Taishans toward all other religions, and especially toward Christianity, was well known all over Japan. No person of any other faith than Shinto had ever been allowed to live in Taisha.

All these things I knew. Yet the call of God in

March 1950 was clear and unmistakable, and His promise was sure: "Be not afraid, but speak, and hold not thy peace: for I am with thee, and no man shall set on thee to hurt thee: for I have much people in this city" (Acts 18:9-10).

I told our missionary, Dr. Eckel, about my call and the compulsion that my wife, Nana, and I felt God had put upon us to go to this pagan city at once.

Dr. Eckel looked very troubled. "I appreciate your earnestness, Koichi-san," he said to me, "and I believe in your call. I am proud of you for your willingness to go to that difficult place. But why don't you wait until your baby comes?"

Nana and I had faced all that. Our first baby was due in five months. Humanly speaking, it would have been better to wait until the child was born. But we had prayed until God's will was clear, and we felt that He was telling us to go at once. I quoted again the promise God had given us (Acts 18:9-10) when He called us.

We counseled and prayed together awhile longer, and then I went home, but the compulsion to go at once continued to press upon Nana and me, so we made our preparations and left as soon as possible for Taisha.

When we got off the train at Taisha, I told Nana that she had better wait in the station while I went to search for a house or a room in which we could live. She prayed while I trudged up and down the streets.

As we had feared, no one would rent us even a tiny space, at any price.

I went back to the station, and we prayed together, reminding God of His call and His promise and asking Him to find us a house. Then I started out again.

Beside one poor house, more dilapidated than the rest, I saw an old woman standing.

"Oba-san [Dear Old Lady]," I said. "Would you please tell me where there is a house for rent?"

She looked startled. "House for rent! Oh, no, no! There is no house for rent in this town. You look like a stranger. You will never find shelter in Taisha."

"I just arrived in town to preach the gospel," I asserted boldly.

"The gospel? What is the gospel?" she inquired curiously.

I told her as briefly and plainly as I could, and I saw by her face that she was interested.

"What about your religion?" I asked.

"Religion is no good!" Her eyes grew dark and angry. "I don't believe in any religion or any god," she cried vehemently. "My husband has been sick for 55 years. He hasn't been able to walk since he was 30 years old. We sought salvation and healing from the 80 million gods of this city, but all we received was poverty. We spent all of our money. No good! No good! We are very poor now. We don't believe in any gods!" She spat on the ground to show her disgust.

As I listened and sympathized with the old woman, I heard God's voice whispering, "I want to help this man."

"I understand how you must feel," I said to the woman. "Would you let me come to see your husband, just for a short time, and pray to my God for him?"

"Do you charge any money for your prayers?" she demanded suspiciously.

"No *Oba-san*. I never charge for prayer. The gospel of Jesus Christ is free for all."

She led the way into her home. It was a typical Japanese house with two rooms, and it must have been at least 150 years old. As we entered the door, a terrible odor came from one of the rooms, which was very dark. I followed the old woman inside, and in a little while I made out a very old man lying on a dirty pallet. His cheekbones stood out sharply in his thin, pale face, and his eyes were sunken. Only one tooth remained in his mouth, and his tongue was twisted from the long years of pain and misery he had endured. The joints of his emaciated legs were swollen and stiff, and he was unable even to turn over.

My heart ached with compassion for the wretched man. I sat down beside him and spoke loud and clear to reach his dim ears, as I told him of Jesus Christ and His power to forgive sin.

The old man listened in astonishment and growing distress.

"Preacher," he gasped, when I had finished, "what shall I do? While I listened to your story of Jesus, I knew I had gone far from the truth. What shall I do? Tell me, Preacher!"

"First of all you must confess your sin before God and repent," I answered. "Then you must receive Jesus Christ as your Savior. You must be born again into the kingdom of God."

"But, Preacher, I am 85 years old now. How can I be born again?"

"Have faith in God. You shall have the new birth and become a new creature in Christ Jesus."

He was filled with the spirit of obedience. He began to confess his sins, revealing the typical wicked life of many men who do not know God. The results of sin in his life were plain, for he had come to spiritual and almost physical death.

When he had made a full confession, he accepted Christ as his personal Savior.

"Will you also now believe in Christ to heal you, *O jii-san* [Dear Old Man]?" I said, bending over him.

"Oh, but that would be impossible," he answered in distress. "I have been like this for 55 years. Nothing, no one, can make me well again now."

"*O jii-san,*" I said again earnestly, "only trust in God. You have lain here in helpless misery and pain for many years, it is true, but now you belong to the true God; He will take care of everything."

A gleam of hope lit up his face. I quoted the

verse from Acts: "Silver and gold have I none; but
such as I have give I thee: In the name of Jesus Christ
of Nazareth rise up and walk" (3:6).

We prayed together fervently, and as we said
"Amen," suddenly the old man's feet and anklebones
received strength, and he leaped up and stood and
walked and praised God!

It was wonderful!

When the old man's wife saw this great miracle
of God, she grasped her head with her hands and
cried, "O true God! O true God! Depart from me,
for I am a sinner!"

But the true God drew closer in love, and as she
prayed and repented and confessed her sins, she, too,
found Christ as her personal Savior.

Back and forth the two old people walked,
weeping and praising God.

"Go and get your wife," they said. "You can live
with us and start your mission in our house. We are
not afraid of the 80 million Shinto gods now."

The story of Kichitaro Nakabayashi's [Kee-chee-
TAH-roe Nah-kah-bah-YAH-shee] healing spread
rapidly through the town. People were astonished,
but they could not deny the miracle, for Kichitaro
himself walked the streets and told them what God
had done for him. Still no one came to ask about the
Christian God, for they were all under the rigid con-
trol of the Shinto priests.

God had answered our first prayer quickly, for

we had found a home and a place for our mission within a few hours after we arrived in Taisha. But we soon discovered that we could not buy food or any other supplies in the city. I went to every store, even the smallest, but each shopkeeper shook his head and said, "We can't help you. You are a Christian. You can't buy anything in this town."

Nana and I prayed much. I tried to send a letter telling of our plight to the Nazarenes in Tokyo, but the postmen were Shintoists. They tore my letter up. Then I tried to take a bus to the next town to buy food, but no one would sell me a bus ticket. Had Kichitaro not found a way to buy rice from time to time, we would all have starved.

Our baby was born one night in September, and we named her *Migiwa* [Mee-GEE-wa (hard g here)], which means "still water side," from the 23rd psalm. As soon as I saw her, I knew that something was wrong. Frightened, I ran a mile to the doctor's home and begged him to come and see my baby.

But he said, "I cannot go to the Christian church. Why don't you bring her up here?"

"I can't," I cried. "She is in a very critical condition. Please, hurry and come with me."

"Oh, I see," he answered calmly. "Well, I can't help you. I suppose your God will take care of your baby so that you will have time. Bring her up here."

I ran back home and wrapped the tiny infant in a blanket. But even as I started the long way back to the doctor's, I saw the color of her face change and knew that her breath had stopped. I went on anyway, hoping that I might be wrong, but I was not.

Coming back from the doctor's with my dead baby, my heart was broken with sorrow. I could not understand why this had happened. I could not see how this could be God's will.

"Why must You take my baby from me?" I cried in anguish. "I came down to Taisha for Your kingdom. Why must You take my first child from me?"

When I thought of my poor wife, my body felt as though it were going to crumble. "Why! Why!" I cried again in despair.

Then in the hushed stillness of the breaking dawn, I heard God's voice: "Except a corn of wheat fall into the ground and die, it abideth alone: but if it die, it bringeth forth much fruit" (John 12:24).

Oh, thank God! He never fails. I took His comforting word to my wife, and together we offered our child to Him in trust and obedience—the best gift we had.

We made a tiny box for Migiwa's casket and a white cross for a grave post.

Migiwa's death broke the barriers that separated us from the people of Taisha.

Many people came to see the funeral. They had never seen a Christian funeral service, and they were curious. Perhaps, too, God's Spirit pricked their hearts because of their harsh treatment of us, for their

faces were more responsive than I had ever seen
them.

That was a good day for evangelism. I preached
the wonderful message of Christ, and at the end of
my preaching three young people came to the altar
and were saved.

Then we lined up for the march to the cemetery,
high on a hill outside of town. It was eight o'clock at
night, and we carried candle lanterns for light. Several
young men asked permission to carry the cross and
casket. When I saw them, my heart was touched, for
they were parolees just out of prison—friendly out-
casts from society. In their own way they were show-
ing their sympathy for Nana and me, who also had
had no friends in this evil city.

Shadowy forms parted in the streets to let our
funeral procession through. One young high school
boy, trying to see what we were, didn't get out of the
way soon enough, and I bumped into him.

"What are you doing here?" he demanded excit-
edly. "What is that cross? I have never seen such a
thing before. Is this a funeral procession?"

His barrage of questions startled me, for I had not
expected it. "Who are you?" I countered in return. "I
am the pastor of the Taisha Church of the Nazarene."

"My name is Tsujimoto [Tsoo-jee-MOH-toe],"
the boy answered. "I was following the procession
because I was curious. It looked very queer to me.
What is that cross?"

"It is the symbol of the true God, who gave His Son on a Cross many years ago to pay the penalty for our sins," I said. The procession stopped while I explained more fully the meaning the Cross could have for Tsujimoto that very night if he wanted it to.

"I do want it to," he said earnestly, when I had finished. "I want Christ to forgive my sins."

And there in the middle of the street that young high school boy gave his heart to God.

Thank God! Before I ever buried my own child, God gave me four spiritual children—the first fruits of the gospel in Taisha.

From that time on, the Christian faith spread rapidly in Taisha until in 1955 there were 150 people coming to the Nazarene Sunday School each Sunday.

Steven Gulley 8-29-02